CW00346092

The Steps Bef

First - create the con

This is the eighth publication by Hollin Books. The others are:-

The Too Busy Trap

Notes on Behavioural Management Techniques, 3rd Edition

How To Escape From Cloud Cuckoo Land, 2nd Edition

How To Empty The Too Hard Box, 2nd Edition

Ideas For Wimps

Behavioural Coaching, 2nd Edition

Behavioural Safety for Leaders

Many thanks to everyone who read the drafts and sent me comments and suggestions, each of whom enhanced the plot in some way. Special thanks to Nicole Gravina who changed the direction of the book in its early stages and also wrote the foreword. I received wise ideas and feedback on the early drafts from Richard Kazbour, Donald Wroe, Lisa Kazbour and Rachel Edwards. My writing process has been massively impacted since Lynn Dunlop became editor in chief, her talent and influence is evident in all the individual steps culminating in the completion of this book.

Thanks to Jean Lees for providing the cover photo and to Kirstie Edwards for the back cover photo.

Special thanks to Joanne Lees for the fabulous, insightful cartoons.

Hollin Publishing
Bollington
Cheshire
SK10 5LF
www.hollinconsulting.co.uk
First published by Hollin Publishing July 2013
Hollin Publishing is a division of Hollin Consulting Ltd
© Copyright 2013 Hollin Consulting Ltd

Graphics by Creative Hero
ISBN 978-0-9563114-9-8

Foreword by Dr Nicole Gravina

Over the years, many leaders have been trained in Behavioral Management Techniques (BMT). Some of them, equipped with the knowledge of behavioral science, go on to make meaningful improvements and have a massive impact on the organizations where they work. Others don't do much at all and many fall somewhere in between. In my experience, the leaders who have a massive impact took the behavioral science they learned and generalized it to all parts of their organization. They were then able to use it to see ten steps ahead on the chess board. Those who had no impact may have been able to state the definitions, but when they looked at the chessboard, they were still reacting to the last move.

My interpretation is that 'the steps before step one' are steps a leader takes to create the conditions for success. These steps are not complex; in fact, they are quite simple and I am convinced that almost anyone could do them if they only made the time to learn and practice. They are the things people do to simultaneously create momentum and reduce drag.

To build momentum, leaders have to start by getting the attention of their people and creating engagement. As Howard describes in this book, they can do this by consistently following up on things, building relationships, increasing upward feedback, and making visible changes that win over the workforce.

On the 'reducing drag' side, Howard explains that leaders have to make it easier for their people to do the right things. They can achieve this by eliminating barriers for success, relentlessly focusing on simple and important goals, and reducing frustration and fear in the workforce.

All of this might sound like the end goal, but it isn't. It's simply what needs to be in place before people can properly focus on improving safety, production, quality, and other results.

Often times, leaders make the mistake of thinking that if they clearly articulate a process and expectations, results will automatically improve. The truth is, leading through overlapping antecedents creates the need to micromanage and produces minimal effort and maximum frustration. An alternative option is to get people engaged and allow them to make improvements. Most of the time we find that involving the right people in the improvement process and creating the conditions for success leads to more and better improvements than we could have imagined. It sounds simple, but it isn't always easy.

I suggest that as you read each chapter, you don't just focus on the specific examples, but rather find ways to generalize the concepts and solutions to your current struggles and goals. A little thought and reflection by the reader will provide endless insight into creating the conditions for success in your part of the world.

Creating momentum and reducing drag is the stuff great leaders do every day and mediocre leaders never think about. Behavioral science is not a process that you follow, it's a way of thinking and doing. This books helps leaders start to see a few steps ahead on the chessboard.

Dr Nicole Gravina, Des Moines, June 2013

Contents

1. Introduction

My old company had a saying: 'ready, fire, aim'. I heard it frequently on projects where, for example, an impatient site engineer was so enthusiastic about building something that he missed a step (or two) out of his preparation. It could put the section of work back a week or so while he went back to start again. His boss would say, "Only this time do it properly."

'Prepare the ground before you plant' is another piece of wisdom that does not fit well with your average impatient type of person, and there are many of them around. I include a number of examples in this book of workplace dysfunction caused by impatience. I have chosen the phrase 'the steps before step one' as the foundation for the book and this is my attempt to argue that it's a good idea to spend a bit more time planning future behaviours before your first visible action. I have extensively used the basic principles of behavioural science to assist my arguments.

The steps before step one will help people understand that just as you wouldn't paint the living room ceiling without first protecting the furniture, speaking out in an unplanned and careless way can lead to problems. Preparing the ground, making sure all the people and physical elements are in place first is the smart thing to do; it's the only way success will be achieved. I will also discuss at length why it is that so many people ignore this key element of being able to win, succeed, be happy, live an enriched life.

When we ask, "Why are you doing that?" the most common response is, "It's the way we do things around here." The second question is usually, "If you could start with a clean sheet of paper would it look like it does now?" and of course the answer is either, "I don't know," or just plain - "No."

We recently had the opportunity of talking to a senior management team who had all been present at the very beginning of quite a large and complex project. Our meeting was held some 18 months after the job kicked off and they were having big problems with meetings and IT. We asked, "Why did you set out to have bad meetings and bad IT?" "We didn't," came the reply. What actually happened was they didn't deliberately set out to have great meetings and great IT; they just let nature take its course, and nature never does us any favours in these matters.

It is possible that over the course of our lives we have been programmed to take lots of the wrong things seriously and lots of the right things lightly. I discuss behavioural debt and its impact on relationships at work. I deal with how common it is for people to do absolutely every behaviour under the sun except the one that is the key behaviour for success. I cover many 'in work' situations and point out stupidity, hypocrisy, mind numbing corporate nonsense, the use of 'old wives' tales' as key business strategy, the heartbreaking stress some people are put under, good and bad examples of remuneration in the workplace, bureaucracy and its corrosive effect on organisations and people alike; it's a roller coaster ride packed with observations that will make you laugh (or cry).

If you have read the previous seven books in the Hollin series then you will recognise the style. If not, I assure you I may be approaching these serious subjects with humour but I am deadly serious in my intent to try to eradicate the more dubious organisational behaviours from the planet. Yes, planet, why not have a big ambition for what is a very big ask?

I was trained in behavioural science by a lovely man called Dr Bill Hopkins and his mantra was, "We need to get behavioural science to the world." A simple but worthy quest. While attending a conference in Atlanta, Georgia, I met another stalwart of the behavioural community called Dr Teodoro

Ayllon. I repeated Bill's mantra to him and he replied, "Yes, that's it, why hasn't it happened already?" It's taken me a while to figure out, but behavioural science in its pure form is not that much use; it needs to be blended with a number of other elements in order for it to work effectively. It's like Microsoft products – we only use 5% of what's available to us, but that's all we need to be effective. This book uses a number of behavioural science terms. I've included a glossary in appendix A describing the ones I've used.

The Steps Before Step One represents the observations, feedback and results of the work carried out by the people in the Hollin team and wider BMT group; we are all actively learning, teaching and coaching. I hope this book helps people link their everyday frustrations with behavioural science so they can learn to solve their own problems, and learn behaviour in the process. BMT is now widely known; over the next few years I am sure it will continue to grow in awareness and popularity. At some point, soon I hope, someone will be able to announce that they got behaviour to the world.

2. Create the conditions for success

If you want to cultivate success, you have to prepare the ground first. The trouble is, preparation is often counter-intuitive, especially to start with. From a behavioural point of view, this is because the result is the end goal, the source of the ultimate reinforcement. Until we learn a better way, it feels right to try and get to the reinforcement as fast as possible and avoid anything that gets in the way.

Acting on intuition is automatic and feels natural. Behaviourally, acting on intuition is very reinforcing: the nature of intuition is that we're sure we'll get the result we want. The fact that we're acting, doing something now, straightaway, adds to the reinforcement. When it comes to matters regarding humans, however, most people's intuition does not help much.

The 'right brain' is associated with the process of intuition; but some people exhibit a 'wrong brain' for sure. People often rely mistakenly on intuition to decide 'next steps' or how to respond to someone else. An intuitive response is automatic; a counter-intuitive response is considering what to say and how to act. While intuitive responses can be inadvertently confrontational, a considered response will be laced with opportunity for discovery. It's the difference between believing the answer is inside of us and thinking the answer is in the environment, if we would only pay attention to it.

We customarily and frequently fail to get what we want because we just blurt it out rather than preparing the ground for success first. It's not as effective asking the kids to go to bed when the TV is still switched on. In the Godfather film, Don Corleone said, "Make sure you get agreement from the heads of all the other families before you ask for something in public." Proverbs, parents, fictional master criminals; what more evidence do you want that preparing the ground is the best way to achieve a successful yield?

Creating the conditions for success is the whole game. The final of the 400 metres race at the Olympics is the result of four or more years of the 'steps before step one'. If your interactions with other people were all well thought through before you acted, how much more effective would you be at getting what you want for yourself, your family and your organisation? I am not talking about hours of preparation here, I am talking about a small consideration before you act, not hours, not minutes, just seconds.

In my experience, the vast majority of destructive behaviours are the verbal ones that are not thought through properly. Turning up to meetings unprepared, making careless promises then forgetting, promising the kids something then reneging, talking over someone else; all common behaviours, all easy to observe, all easy to fix if you can create the conditions to fix them. Think of all the things you could do to increase your chances of success before you act. Consider a number of steps and choose one. Try it out, observe what happens and look at the result. Adjust your responses and try again. This process of iteration is a very powerful tool; it is Darwin's theory of evolution and it works very well indeed. It just takes two things which don't come naturally to most of us: a little patience and persistence.

3. Without engagement

Persistence and patience are important factors but without engagement I am afraid you have nothing to work on. People may be ignoring you for no particular reason. I know it doesn't feel like that, but that's the effect. One key conversation can win you some attention, from your boss, your children or a complete stranger.

Knowing what to say and when to say it is a highly learnable skill. I have coached people many times to think about what they will say at the impending meeting; write some ideas down. You know the protagonists, you know what they are probably going to say, how they will react; think of some lines before you get to the meeting. Then all you have to do is say them, you don't have to worry about thinking of something cool to say. You already did that; most of the work is done. You just have to say the words.

Do many people do this? No, they don't, and here are some reasons:-

1. Most of the people I advise are well into the red on the 'too busy trap'. They perceive that it will take too much time.
2. Most folks don't like writing down potential things they could say on a piece of paper, even in the safety of their own privacy.

3. The spectre of fear generated in some work places is so great
    that it paralyses the performer into deciding that they will go
    for the safety of doing what they always did instead of doing
    the right thing, or at least something different.

There is a YouTube clip making the rounds featuring Bob
Newhart. He plays a therapist solving people's problems and
the woman in the clip explains her behaviour to him. He shouts,
"Stop it!" then charges her $5 for his time. The humour is
derived by the fact that, though an obvious thing to say, it could
never work because therapists have to create engagement with
their client before they can be effective. In fact the 'creating
engagement' phase is probably the most time-consuming phase
and could take months, even years. How I yearn to be able to
wave a magic wand and have unchallenged understanding and
engagement with my clients.

"How do I get engagement with this plant manager," asked a
colleague. "He is mostly solitary, attends meetings, says very
little, when he says 'enough', that's the end of the conversation.
He won't meet me. He has birthday lunches with people from
the plant and that's how he gains his view of the mood within
the plant. We have all kinds of anonymous data from our
courses which describe plenty of opportunities for
improvements, but this guy doesn't want to see it. He doesn't
respond to my emails or those of his safety manager. What can
we do?" "On your own, not a lot," was my response. This kind
of manager, firmly set in 'comfortable delusion', is very
difficult to budge. The only way it can happen is if the people
who work for him get together and create a shaping plan for
engagement: This could inject some guile and bravery into the
situation. We can always suggest ideas for guile but we cannot
provide surrogate bravery.

Getting together with a group of people and coming up with ideas of things you could say and do is a lot of fun. In fact, you could make it part of interactions at coffee, lunch, in meetings etc. If what you are doing is exploring new ways of creating engagement with someone then, over time, just like anything else, you will get very good at it. Creating engagement is like any other kind of learning, it accelerates with practice. I have talked many times about the line 'is there any reason you wouldn't take feedback from somebody like me?' It works really well.

Here are some other lines you could try:-

1. "I have a couple of suggestions for how we could run parts of the plant differently; would you like to hear them?"
2. "I have a couple of suggestions about how we run meetings; would you like to hear them?"
3. "Do you have something particular on your mind these days?"
4. "Could I give you some feedback? It's a bit sensitive."
5. "Are you happy with reporting/safety/payments/invoicing/whatever right now?"
6. "Do you think the mood in the camp has dropped over the last few weeks?"
7. "Do you think the mood here has picked up in the last few weeks?"

Perhaps it would be useful here to step down one more level of detail. You could take one of the suggestions from above, write some possibilities of things you could say on this theme and rate them from too strong to too weak, producing a range of potential statements. Number 4 above is – "Could I give you some feedback? It's a bit sensitive." Maybe a range of statements could be:-

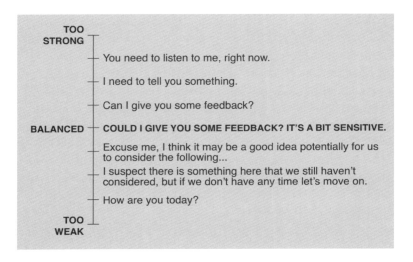

```
TOO
STRONG ┬
       ┼  You need to listen to me, right now.

       ┼  I need to tell you something.

       ┼  Can I give you some feedback?

BALANCED ┬ COULD I GIVE YOU SOME FEEDBACK? IT'S A BIT SENSITIVE.

       ┴  Excuse me, I think it may be a good idea potentially for us
          to consider the following...
       ┴  I suspect there is something here that we still haven't
          considered, but if we don't have any time let's move on.
       ┼  How are you today?
TOO  ┴
WEAK
```

As you can see, the first and last may not get the result you're after. It's worth writing down extremes of things to say because it helps put problems into perspective and gives options of things that could be said. This allows a more considered approach. Yes, this takes time but some people have been stuck on the same square of the board for many years. A few minutes' planning can relieve many years' angst. The golden rule of creating engagement is that we all operate on our environment. The big boss and little old me; when we are both in the room, I can have as much influence over proceedings as he/she can. A disengaged boss is unlikely to have prepared for a meeting with you, so all you have to do is think of something unexpected to say.

This is why Sunflowers[1] do so well; they are smart enough to set themselves on a path of looking good. In some organisations *looking good* is much easier than *being good*, you understand. Looking good also carries with it all the lack of trust and respect issues trailing most Sunflowers. One thing you have to compliment successful Sunflowers on is that the best of them have mastered engagement. It's cynical engagement, but at least it exists.[2]

Engagement for selfish reasons is not such a bad starting point if the overall endgame is to improve the business, enrich others' lives and spread the word on the use of behavioural science to improve the world. Dr Bill Redmon used to say, "I have a quest, I have an honourable goal, I'll take any form of transport that will get me there." If the initial engagement carries with it the odd sunflower tendency, then we are all human; a bit of flattery can get you a long way. At some point, hopefully early on, you'll have to be tough if you are to get to the right place in the right way. You will eventually have to demonstrate determination, strength and integrity, and these qualities are very attractive to followers.

---

[1] Sycophants at work are like sunflowers: they look beautiful and golden to those above them, but are spiky and ugly from below.

[2] There's a common downside to the Sunflower strategy of getting on in business. Even the leaders will eventually notice that Sunflowers do not exhibit any courage. They will be passed over for key jobs, especially when they enter the 'top level' business arenas. Yes, I agree that there are plenty of sycophants appointed to boards of directors simply to vote with the CEO; this is cynical, there's a lot of it about. Over time I believe we could make this kind of greedy outlook unfashionable at least.

4. It's the environment, stupid!

Creating engagement isn't just about what you say; the environment you choose to say it in is important as well. In behavioural speak, the environment is the room and the people within it, it's the home and the people within it, it's the factory, the train, the aeroplane, the car, the football stadium, the doctor's surgery, the bus, the theatre, the shop, AND the people within. If you are a living person then you are always part of an environment. We all have a space around us, it may or may not contain other people; it's our environment.

The environment we are in drives our behaviour. Our behaviour changes as the environment changes. We 'operate on our environment', that is, our behaviour is contingent on whatever environment we find ourselves in. In familiar environments our behaviour normalises into what we call habits and what the experts in behavioural science call 'conditioned responses over time'. When presented with a choice, the science tells us that we will take the most reinforcing option. If we find the most reinforcement by responding to people's requests in a timely fashion and honouring our obligations, then over time, in other people's eyes, we gain a reputation for someone with integrity. It's easy!

It is said that the leader creates the environment and the leader gets what the leader deserves. It's true in most cases. Good planning creates good workplace environments and it's quite a responsibility. As an engineer I am familiar with planning: You can't pour the concrete until the steel is fixed, you can't fix the steel without a base to work off, and you will also need steel-fixers and steel and many other things that planners of construction get good at forecasting over time. The feedback in the environment during a reinforced concrete project is live and immediate: no concrete, no job. Physical feedback is commonplace and it's what stops us placing our hand on the hot stove; it's what motivates us to put the rubbish out for the collection on the right day.

The environment is also packed full of other, arguably more important feedback. There is a multiplicity of feedback between humans. High levels of honest feedback are rare because everyone holds back or controls what they say in order to remove all the risks learned via their history with those around them. It's a question of balance. A stranger can walk in and see the elephant; it's been there for a while but everyone else had filtered it out. Of course, this filtering is in place in order to get to the end of the day with the minimum amount of stress, which equates to the maximum amount of available reinforcement.

5. Little shards of feedback

It would be wonderful if feedback abounded in a frequent and skilful manner, backwards and forwards in a mutually beneficial way to help us all with our lives. The small birds in my garden get their feedback in regular doses; they collect food, make nests, rear young and do the same next year. That is, as long as the predators don't get them or their fledglings. In contrast, much feedback to humans is received in little shards. It makes us think, 'well, I'm not going to say that again' or 'do that again'. Nature delivers consequences that teach us what will work and what will not work in any given situation, but to be most effective we need more than that.

Feedback is the basis on which we learn. If we don't get any feedback, we don't learn. Receiving robust feedback is a key tenet of the steps before step one. Setting up robust feedback loops for yourself will mean you have a good read on what's going on around you. Without a good read on what's going on and what people are saying about you, well, it's akin to playing chess wearing a space suit; every time you make a move your big gloves knock some of the other chess pieces over.

Many people behave in ways we think are outrageous. These people didn't receive the feedback (if it was delivered at all).

Our reluctance to deliver honest and accurate feedback is tempered by our need to avoid confrontation and also avoid upsetting someone else. Of course, we rationalise our behaviour a lot, and justify our actions to ourselves to make us feel better. When I say we do that frequently, we do it a lot; if you tie a piece of string on your finger to remind you to look out for this, you won't have long to wait.

So what are we left with? There is the stuff we know about other people that we don't deliver and there's all the other stuff that is broadcast around us every day that we can observe. Let's call these 'incoming' and 'outgoing'. Also, there are potential 'test balloons' we could be sending out to check our assumptions and feel more confident about how we can effectively deliver some feedback.

I've been listening to some old Van Morrison records lately, recorded in the times before digital recording when the band played live. They are littered with lots of minor losses of timing, lapses in intonation, and losses of groove. They evoke memories of course, but there is also a charm associated with imperfection; it's honest and has character.

I have had the pleasure of spending time in recording studios back in the good old days and also very recently. A missed note or late note played these days can be fixed on the recording with a quick flash of the mouse; it's very tempting to make the repair. One thing for sure about playing with musicians - there is tons of reinforcement. From the playing and from the other people involved, it's pleasurable, it feels great. The feedback between musicians was always there. In the old days we compromised; these days we don't have to so we don't. The ultimate product now is different, but the pleasure of playing with other musicians has not changed; it's still fantastic.

THE   STEPS   BEFORE   STEP   ONE

In the recording studio there is plenty of incoming and outgoing feedback, it's the holy grail of a 'feedback rich environment'. You really don't have to work hard to receive feedback in certain creative environments. Musicians have a certain raised-eyebrow look, a glance at whoever just played a great note or moved the rhythm in a certain way; it's a great feeling when it happens, it's genuine, it's very reinforcing. Our BMT gang do the same when someone in the group says something interesting, creative or funny. It sounds cheesy I know, but it does feel great; it's teamwork.

Creating this kind of environment at work would guarantee high performance, so how do we do that? We have to take the little shards of feedback currently in the environment and adjust them in order to increase the frequency of the good stuff, the reinforcing stuff.

1. Take a reading on the feedback in the environment, incoming and outgoing.
2. Test out the environment for its ability to receive new feedback.
3. Adjust the dose and frequency of outgoing feedback.
4. Keep your radar at full power to detect new incoming feedback.
5. Adjust your feedback and iterate this process.
6. Celebrate when you nail something.

On the other side of this feedback coin, I have some experience of what you might call 'high power' meetings. Senior people in a politically charged meeting with a number of personal agendas at play. Prior to the meeting I have a think about each character and what they might say. Most people in a typical Machiavellian cast will be trying to achieve something, fair or foul. I note down what I think they might say and what I could say as a retort. I will make a list and take it to the meeting. I would say I am right about 40% of the time; I usually use 4 out of 10 of my prepared retorts. Most people will not take the trouble to prepare in this way. I do, because it works.

If I sit in meetings I am always on the lookout for personal agendas. A lot of them are dead giveaways. My friends who read the draft of this book suggested I gave some examples so here they are - first the stereotypical label for the act and then the act, despicable or otherwise:-

1. Passive aggressive – When you are talking, people are looking at their phones or some other distraction. Take a look if they are doing it while the boss is speaking.
2. Bullying boss – "I know how many tons we got yesterday, how many tons did we get the day before? You don't know? Go and find out, you should know everything about your project."
3. Disorganised – "Only half the people are here, should we give them 10 minutes?"
4. Exclusion – "Yes, I agree it's a serious subject but I think we should discuss this with a different cast of attendees."
5. The poisoned chalice – "I have to go now; Howard would you mind reading through my next report to the team, please?"
6. One-upmanship – "I am very sorry everyone, but I now have to leave to go to a very important meeting in another building."
7. Assumption of support – "I think there are a number of us around the table that don't agree with that."
8. Politically correct delaying tactic – "I don't think we are in full possession of all the facts here. Why don't we ask for more information and carry on the discussion at the next meeting?"
9. Association – "Yes, I hear there are some people up to no good. I believe they are friends of yours, Howard?"
10. Railroading – After you have spoken someone says, "Well I think we have more than aired that subject; what's next?"
11. Using mystery – "Yes, I think we all know why that was bound to happen."

12. Marginalisation – "We all appreciate your typically northern sense of humour, Howard."
13. Put down – "Correct me if I'm wrong here, but have you ever delivered any projects in the nuclear industry, Howard?"
14. Not doing the steps before step one – "I'm sorry I haven't had chance to read the minutes of the last meeting, could someone catch me up?"
15. Feedback starved meetings – Ones that run without opportunity for people to vote anonymously on the subjects discussed.
16. Out of control leader – He turns up to a meeting with people a few layers below him in the organisation and demands certain actions, right away.
17. Intimidation – "Yeah, we've spent too long on other items today; Howard could you just rattle through your bit in two minutes please?"
18. Betrayal – You say the thing you and your mates agreed you would say and they don't support you like they said they would.
19. Stealing the show to take the limelight, coupled with marginalising comment – "I am sorry everyone, but I have to go now. I have some reservations, but in general I support Mr Lees and all he is doing here."
20. Predator – "This garden is cram-packed full of young fledglings, yummy."
21. Questions you're never going to ask at the start of meetings – "Hey everyone, could we go round the table and could you just let us all know what preparation you did for this meeting beforehand?"

It's all in good humour you understand, but how would you respond to these examples if they were fired at you in a meeting?

6. Mutually beneficial amnesia

I have travelled many times on aeroplanes, lots of long-distance, overnight flights. Of course, many flights suffer from frequent turbulence, so there you are, you have just woken up with a desire to use the lavatory and you note the seatbelt sign is lit. Sod it, you think. I need a pee. I will break this rule. You are just entering the lavatory and the cabin crew look at you and smile. I need a pee, the crew don't want to clear up a mess; mutually beneficial amnesia. The workplace is also a popular location for everyone conveniently forgetting stuff. Sometimes it's prompted by an irritating rule that nobody wants to adhere to and sometimes by a person flaunting the rules that you can't be bothered calling them on.

The safety arena is a very common place where people observe and ignore; it's how some work places get incredibly dangerous. Bit by bit, inch by inch, standards are whittled away. The next minute someone is saying, "Yeah, watch that ladder, it's got a rung missing," or "I forbid you to have another injury on this site for thirty days," or very scarily, "As long as the wind stays in the west, we'll be OK." These comments are all genuine, they were all spoken by someone. The last comment was stated some hours before a refinery exploded with considerable loss of life.

One of the most harmful examples of mutually beneficial amnesia centres on the use of business processes. An awful lot of misconception about the basics of how to run an organisation lies around written processes. Just because all conceivable events have been covered in a set of rules does not mean anyone has read them or that anyone will adhere to them. Many leaders will quote the rules as if everyone is working to them, even though they know damn well they are not. Taking it as read that the act described in the process will occur and be skilfully delivered is one of the dumbest assumptions in business. The writers of the rules could spend more time in the boat at sea with the rowers and get a better understanding of the reality of the work environment.

I suspect most groups of people who gather together also include various sizes of 'elephants in the room' - things we are all aware of but no-one mentions: it's been here so long we have stopped noticing. The reason for this is that the people in the room have all either consciously or subconsciously detected the possibility for punishment in the form of conflict. Humans seek out reinforcers and avoid punishers. They do this all the time; channel hopping, beating someone else in the queue for food or boarding a plane, competing in meetings, beating the kids at games. These examples are varied I know, and some are trivial, some are dysfunctional, but I would not underestimate what lengths people will go to win reinforcers and avoid punishers. Many people disregard the trivial aspect of these actions and still try to win, even if relationships they value are damaged in the process.

The road to recovery is paved with gold. This gold is already available and bountiful; it comes in the form of feedback. Honest, insightful and skilfully delivered feedback; something you cannot have until you have created the conditions which will ensure that you get this golden feedback. You probably have a

lot of apologising to do! All this mutually beneficial amnesia
that we have been party to has in effect reduced the chances
that our version of us is not the same as everyone else's.
We mortgage our future behaviour by avoiding the truth today.

The mutually beneficial amnesia is helpful now, but it might not
be in the future. The silly examples of behaviours in planes or
shops are interesting but not damaging. It's the more subtle stuff
that occurs at work that needs to receive more consideration.
I have coached leaders to ask in meetings, "Is there an elephant
in the room?" Of course, this kind of scary question has to be
asked a number of times before you can rid yourselves of the
amnesia that's built up over time. One day, maybe someone
will ask, "Do we have any mutually beneficial amnesia out
there folks?"

There are moments, emotional moments when someone says
something you didn't expect, in a way you don't appreciate
and you respond defensively, even aggressively. If you screw
up at the very time you should be responding well, you can
still apologise. Apologising costs you nothing, a tiny bit of
perceived pride maybe. You will be a better person for doing so.

7. Develop respect - don't be afraid of those key conversations

Most people I know have some behavioural roadblock in their lives that they are stuck on. It could be a tendency to eat or drink too much, leaving things to the last minute, not ringing someone back, tolerating someone else's irritating behaviour (for many years in some cases). It could be as simple as letting an expensive insurance bill roll on to the next year incurring a higher premium, not clearing the leaves out of the grid, not checking your tyre pressure often enough. It could be as serious as keeping key information from your family, hoping a problem will go away while knowing it will be much worse for you when it inevitably gets out.

I would suggest that everyone has a 'respect' and attendant 'trust' score for all their relationships with family, close friends, work colleagues and acquaintances, including people who infrequently pass their orbit. This respect and trust score will be the result of many (mostly) verbal interactions over many years. These interactions will have created your view of the relationship. If you are paying attention to their behaviour then you will have an inkling as to their opinion of you, and how much they trust and respect you.

If you have prepared well, you could probably deliver some feedback to all the people mentioned above. If you have their best intentions in mind, you could probably help them. I am sure you do this anyway. I would ask if you have any idea what the gap is between the amount of help you could give them against the amount you actually give. It is paradoxical, but the very act that will strengthen people's relationships (the delivery of important feedback) is the very thing people shy away from. As the song goes – "You always hurt the one you love, the one you shouldn't hurt at all."

If you have a particular person in mind, perhaps you could write down the things you think they know and the things they don't. Some of these things will be trivial. If you wrote them down, though, the chances are that they are important. There will also be reasons why you have not mentioned many of these things in the past. These reasons will often be your rationalisations rather than what's best for the other person.

If you take the trouble to have these key conversations and they are delivered and received well, then the levels of mutual respect will increase. But hey, if it was this simple you would have done it already, so what are the steps before step one? You probably need help with writing the list and you will definitely need some help and time to consider what to say. I suggest you find someone you can trust. If you can't think of anyone readily then perhaps you need to make a list of people who could help you with this. Of course you can enlist an independent person and do it that way, but finding people you can trust is a key step for the future; it's best to work at that.

8. Verbal behaviours in the workplace, part 1

Having key conversations is important, but gathering data on what others say in the workplace can be very enlightening as well. If the culture is the cumulation of behaviours in the whole organisation, and environment is the effect of the immediate location and the people within, then it's possible to get a feel for the local culture by observing the verbal behaviours in any given location. It is difficult to draw any scientific conclusions with culture as it is too wide, uncontrolled and diverse to conclude anything scientifically accurate. For sure, you can generalise and stereotype; this can be fun and interesting, but it's probably not scientific enough to be a viable BMT tool.

If people have been working in the same place for a number of years then most of the environment-creating behaviours will be verbal behaviours. Multiple relationships will exist and their characteristics will mostly be a result of the verbal behaviours between people and their responses over time. Imagine you are sat at your desk in your office or cubicle. Some of the time you will be working at a computer, sometimes answering the telephone, chatting with the people around you, chatting in the kitchen, at lunch, with single or multiple numbers of people, spending time in meetings; all of these interactions make up the local culture.

Even in a generally bureaucratic governmental organisation there will be pockets of efficiency and enlightenment and I am sure that even within the successful British cycling team there will be elements of ineffective verbal encounters. In order to use BMT effectively, it's important to create a field of vision that can in some way deliver scientific outcomes. After all, the leverage and the power of this tool comes with the delivery of objective data. So where can we observe these humans in their natural environment and see what they are up to? Well, the most obvious place to start is meetings.

It is very common for senior managers to dismiss meetings as an area that should be observed, even in organisations where more than 50% of people's time is spent in meetings. Of course, that is an early clue as to what we will find if we sit in and make some observations. The Hollin team recently sat in a meeting and created a check list of what we think is useful meeting observation fodder:-

A meeting is a gold mine for gathering data because:-

1.   It's a target-rich zone of verbal behaviours.
2.   It's one of the only places that people interact face-to-face with the other people on the team/project, including the people they don't like.
3.   This is the place where relationships are built; what happens downstream is a product of what happens in these meetings.
4.   It's like standing on stage; it's a chance to observe leadership behaviours in front of the team all at once.
5.   It's one of the only opportunities you get to observe the leadership behaviours of your team.
6.   It's an opportunity to test for understanding and knowledge.
7.   You can test that your messages are reaching your colleagues.

8. It's your chance to ask open questions regarding people rather than just operational detail.
9. It's the best place to look for clues for where to look next.
10. If you can't get something simple like meetings right, how are you going to effectively manage anything else?

Observing meetings - here are some ideas for your preparation before the meeting:-

1. First meeting – just observe, stay in the background.
2. Over time see if you can introduce some consequences to change behaviour – ask if it's possible to run a Radio Frequency (RF) voting session at the end of the meeting (maybe at the beginning too, for compare-and-contrast purposes).
3. Ask if you can record the meeting. A recorder is one of a number of physical items that can affect behaviours and change consequences in meetings.
4. Observe a collection of meetings.
5. Create a location map of where people sit. Make a simple graphic tally every time someone speaks.

Basic data at each meeting - I would suggest these are the basic minimum goals for every meeting:-

1. Housekeeping; did the meeting start and finish on time, was the agenda prepared and followed?
2. Have people prepared for the meeting?
3. Gather data on the close-out of actions from the last meeting.
4. Have people turned up with something to say, without just improvising?
5. Number of attendees, who contributed and how much?

Things to look out for - here are a number of things that you can observe which will provide you with information you can use to get you to the next step and onward from there:-

1. Is someone sending things off-piste?
2. Can you observe leaders, passengers, marginalisers, sunflowers, disrupters, heroes, diffusers, pacifiers, survivors? What are they saying? Can you provide pinpoints for all these labels?
3. Are people on phones calls, texts, email?
4. Is anyone whispering conversations with the person next to them?
5. Are two people having an overt exclusive conversation; discussing something that is irrelevant to others or that others can't join in on? Are there any other power plays?
6. Are two people talking at the same time, and who?
7. Is one person dominating the meeting?
8. How often is the meeting interrupted from outside?
9. Are there any disengaged people? Looking out of the window, doodling etc.
10. Is anyone using "yes but," "no," or "however" at the start of their sentences? (Marshall Goldsmith)
11. Can you detect 'delusion of client'? Does someone in the room appear to be trying to control things by virtue of their power through payment?
12. Is there an elephant in the room? Can you pinpoint it?
13. Do there appear to be any weird, unusual, strange or illogical customs in these meetings?
14. Can you detect confidence, surety, determination, enlightenment, upbeat moods, or positive elements within the meeting and can you pinpoint them? Or the opposite of these?
15. Can you detect elements of trust, or the opposite?
16. Can you detect if bad news is shared and how it is received?
17. Can you detect the focus of the meeting: strategic / operational / tactical? What's getting the most attention?
18. Do people seek out dissenting opinions? How is this done?
19. How are safety and risk being addressed?

9. Verbal behaviours in the workplace, part 2

I don't know anyone who has been trained specifically in the delivery of positive verbal behaviours. Understanding consequences is one thing but writing out sentences and then adjusting them to create the maximum impact is over the top, surely? No, 'sales' training has been designing scripts embracing that kind of scrutiny for many years. I now believe that much leader-thinking needs to be directed at precisely what to say, the exact structure of the sentence. When successfully delivered, the speaker can walk away in the knowledge that they had decided on a form of words and had given the words some thought prior to delivery. I have experienced working for people who consider what they are going to say in the knowledge that everyone is listening to them. It's a great feeling. I worked for some great leaders; I was lucky, most folks are not so lucky.

Here are some examples of words I have encouraged some leaders to say to their people:-

1. I want you to know that I would really like to be effective at helping you in your current role.
2. If you think you are drowning, please let's talk about what we can do to fix it.

3. Do you need any help coaching your people?
4. Can I help simplify things for you?
5. I just want you to know that I think being 'too busy' is a bad thing.
6. If you are too busy then what effect do you think that's having on your people?
7. Do you think you are including enough thinking time into your day?
8. What do you think should be different; what would improve the quality of your day, week, month?
9. Is your diary too full of meetings?
10. What do you think of other people's meetings?
11. What would you do now if you could wave a magic wand and have anything you want? (……..and hope it's not to make you disappear.)
12. If there was an opposing view regarding what we are doing right now, what do you think it might be?

You will notice that none of the examples above are 'operational'. For example:-

How's the programme? What's the state of the rebuild? How much is the value of the claim? How many got off the production line yesterday? Is the team hard at work? Don't forget to tell me if anyone is habitually late or off sick a lot. Have you finished off the report I asked you to submit by tomorrow? These kinds of questions are not only 'operational' but will probably create some kind of aversion over time; they certainly will not create a strong, robust relationship if they represent the majority of interactions with the boss.

A note of caution – It's unlikely that any of the questions and statements would produce desired responses if the right relationship does not already exist. As you can imagine, the right relationship has to be established first: this is the step before step one. I am arguing that a strong, robust and generally honest relationship is a good thing if you want to enjoy someone else's company and work with them for any length of time. I am not sure 'always totally honest' is desirable – consider how that might affect the relationship...

If you have the best interests of the relationship at heart, asking open questions is a good strategy. Here are some more questions you can ask people regarding their career/organisation:-

1. What are you looking for out of your work?
2. Do you have the right recipe just now to get what you want?
3. Is there anything that's disappointing you right now?
4. Would you say you are generally in a positive place at work?
5. Do you feel as if you are punching below your weight right now?
6. Do you think the people around you are successful?
7. Do you find yourself mostly talking about operational stuff or people stuff?

Here are some statements we prepared for a client. The purpose was to see if their directors would honestly respond to these points regarding safety:-

1. I seek out dissenting opinion on safety issues when we plan our work.
2. My safety advisors are coaches, not cops.
3. I 'one-to-one' coach my people:-
    1. weekly
    2. fortnightly
    3. monthly

4. The last conversation I had with a direct report focused primarily on:-
    1. them
    2. production
    3. safety
5. The last conversation I had with my boss focused primarily on:-
    1. them
    2. production
    3. safety
6. I am comfortable that all our people get the support they need managing our client's desires for excessive safety paperwork.
7. I have done a really good job at supporting my people through their improvement plans.
8. Our reporting focuses on lead indicators as much as it needs to.
9. I always return phone calls and emails within a reasonable time.
10. I always personally apologise to people if I have to cancel appointments.

Of course, we already had the data from people in each division, so it was easy to give the directors a 'behavioural index' score showing what they thought they did versus what their people thought. It's unfortunate, but this kind of direct survey is only going to work with an enlightened company.

10. Current strategy – future strategy

It is customary when new businesses or new projects are in the planning stage for people to start off with organisation charts. They map out a system of processes which, in theory, will deliver the business/project. People are given a scope of work and a division or part of the whole to manage and then asked to produce a series of plans to show how they will be delivered. It is agreed that there will be monthly meetings, weekly meetings, monthly reports, weekly reports, agendas are circulated and hey presto, a bureaucracy is born.

The counter-strategy to this is to view the business/project as a continuum of activities, left to right on the page and to manage the interfaces between activities in order to deliver the business/project. The lean community would favour this non-silo, go with the flow approach. Of course, it does not satisfy the traditional organisational needs of status, which drive pay, conditions and all the usual products of a hierarchy. If we were to also think about a behaviourally-sound strategy then we would not want to create any places where hierarchy would overrule good sense. We would not want to be constrained by horizontal process. We would not want anyone to feel constrained in any way. We would not want to be all constipated up with bureaucracy.

I have asked a number of my clients, "When you set this up, how did you go about making sure all meetings were worthwhile, well managed and added value?" I usually get blank faces because it's not a part of the usual strategy of setting up something new. If we are in organisational land rather than production land then most of the behaviours will be verbal. Figuring out how to make sure verbal behaviour in the workplace is going to be positive, contributory to production and also creative is a key deliverable. This is mostly overlooked when setting up a new business/project. It is unusual for mature organisations to 'start again from a clean sheet of paper' for obvious reasons.

It is a common fallacy that processes are the 'hard' components and managing people's behaviours are the 'soft' skills. In my experience most people rely on processes because they are easy. It's easy to write down what you want, it's easy to write utopian procedures and shoehorn them into contracts. It's easy to say, "This is what we want, this is when we want it delivered, this is how you will be paid, this is the quality required, you must turn up to work all neat and tidy, your shirts must be pressed, take your shoes off when you come into the house." It's easy to make these demands. Some are useful, some are pointless; we will all judge which are which ourselves.

The enlightened approach to delivering business/projects invites everyone that will take part in its delivery to also take part in the planning; deciding the detailed components and timescales. I have heard many people talk about this 'we need to make time to get together before we act' stage but not many organisations actually plan it into their processes. A current major project in London has a 'post-contract-award, pre-start' phase where the right people sit down with the right amount time to plan the job properly. This is rare.

A collaborative approach works really well; all the brains working to deliver the business/project. This way, trust is likely to be generated and if that develops then discretionary effort from all the participants will not be far behind. You can't beat a group of motivated, hard-working people to deliver great results.

11. Be generous; people will notice that you care

There is one particular client where quite a mean-spirited culture has developed, just over the last few years. I would argue it's a product of changing the business too much too soon, underestimating just how long people need to bed in new relationships. The 10% rule is great, i.e. every successful reorganisation/restructure recognises that the key to achieving successful change is 90% focused on deployment and 10% on content. It's 'how' it's done not 'what' is done that should be the main focus of the change. Also, people seem to underestimate that the style of leadership required for change is not the same as the style required for sustainable success.

I do struggle to get leaders to apologise; it's tough for some people to see the real impact of their behaviour on others. I have recommended this act many times. I will say, "If you publish the report on the findings on your culture and just apologise, it will offer you an opportunity to start afresh." Most leaders want to be taken seriously; they want people to respect them, they want people to 'vote' for them. Many, however, do not understand where they stand with people; they believe that their people care about them when in many cases they do not. I am sure you can pause for thought and decide which of your bosses, past and present, you cared about, or not.

If you can be generous with your time, respectful with your responses, honour your obligations and remember all the things you should be reinforcing, there is a good chance you can achieve your goal. The good leaders always exhibit a bedrock of basic simple behaviours aligned with setting up trust and respect. Of course they are usually very confident and self assured as well; exhibiting the correct leader behaviours is the very thing that helps you become confident. It feels great when you do the right thing and the result is successful. Doing the right thing in the right way and getting the right result is the goal; anything else is going to be a compromise.

Every now and again you see people succeed by fluke. It happens, it's not the rule, it's the exception. In the same way, you could smoke cigarettes all your life and live to 90. There are examples of this, but the rule says the best way to achieve longevity is to have a healthy lifestyle. There are some people who have amazing charisma and can make a success of even the most dubious propositions. They are not the rule; I know some, but not many.

Many people do not naturally have the style to skilfully deliver briefings to groups; some people seem to shy away from talking to groups. Many people these days would much prefer to send a message via email than talk to another person at all, especially if the message contains anything remotely confrontational. I guess we all know what it feels like to be talked at in an insulting way. Most people do not react well to a 'jobsworth'. No-one enjoys being supervised, especially by someone they don't like. Many people are in desperate need of some training on how to talk to other people and deliver the desired result. You don't necessarily have to care about the person you are talking to, but you do need to be aware of the impact you are having when you do.

It's easy to observe someone who is being careful, even generous, with the way they are addressing other people. It is also easy to observe artless verbal behaviour. Focusing on the goal can be a good principle, but if it diverts the style of delivery to a place where the goal is not going to be achieved, then it is counterproductive. Recognising this hazard and taking practical steps to address it is a very important role of leaders. If in doubt, it is helpful just asking yourself, "What's actually happening here?"

12. The first steps

Dysfunction is inadvertently designed into many organisational procedures. Company initiatives such as 'don't walk by' (a hazard), safety inductions, tool box talks, company briefings, monthly messages from the CEO, emailed announcements to 'all staff', forced ranking, annual appraisals etc. have probably been designed to make the future better, but all have the potential to make the future worse if not skilfully delivered. Of course, all of the above could be delivered skilfully and achieve their intended output. Most standard company procedures have not been sense-checked by someone who understands behavioural science. Most leaders do not check that what was intended actually occurred. Just checking that the process was adhered too is not the same as making sure the original intention of the procedure was delivered.

Some leaders insist that they need to know everything that's going on in their organisation and that they need to know straight away, as it happens. Many meetings and procedures for reporting are predicated on this septic focus; much effort goes in to the collecting of data to feed these beasts (both human and foolscap). Of course these bosses fill themselves with information, some relevant, most not. They still get regular surprises and usually respond badly to them. I have tried to

explain to many of them that the surprises will continue,
forever. You cannot know everything; it's ludicrous to think you
can. This 'need to know everything' is one of the most silly and
stress-creating situations in business.

The leader's primary job is to bring the best out in their people.
Most people would agree with that. The actual value in an
organisation is delivered by the people in that organisation.
The greatest proportion of actual monetary value or service
delivery is probably delivered by the majority of the people in
the organisation. The directors are in a minority in most
organisations, therefore their impact needs to be inspired, artful
and strategic. It needs to be delivered with great skill and the
strategy needs to be simple enough for everyone to understand
what it is and what their part in the delivery of it is.

I do not encounter many organisations at the 'best in class' stage
of this leadership process. Most are doing their best, but have a
mistaken view on the genuine value gained by focusing on
organisational structure, process and activity. Hardly any have a
good understanding of behavioural science and how they could
very simply improve their workplace culture with a few tweaks
here and there.

If the leadership have a true field of vision of what's really
going on everywhere in the organisation then there is a good
chance they are making informed decisions. If the leadership
have created a positive environment then there is a good chance
honesty abounds. If not, there is a good chance aversive
conditions exist.

13. Cycles of abuse

We run many surveys; we use them to gain information on people's aspirations and opinions and we also receive solid data. We analyse the information and share the results of the surveys with our clients, who respond very well or very badly and all the reactions in between these extremes. Sometimes we withhold information or opinion from surveys in the best interests of the people involved, including ourselves. If we receive feedback from a survey that seems to point to an aversive culture then it is usual for this news to be received badly by the leadership. After all, we already have information that says this is likely to happen.

What can we do for this client who has paid for a survey? They may well have said at the outset that they are robust and can take any feedback; they usually do say that. In order to satisfy the rules of shaping we have to pitch our report at a level that will get their attention, but not so strong that we get fired or their people get punished for being honest. It's a matter of judgement on our part. We have been here many times, and we already know that some senior people are going to get upset, stressed and threatened by our report on their culture.

We also know that they will exhibit some or all of the usual defensive responses – discredit the report, the writers, the method of data-collection, the questions, and the observed sound-bites. Rationalise their own circumstances to be victims of a greater plot. See the situation as merely a temporary blip. Question our motives. They might withhold the report from publication or insist they edit it before it is published. They might prevaricate and set up future confirmation amongst their people that the survey was yet another sham designed to lift everyone's hopes only for them to be dashed, as usual. They may, in extreme circumstances, see the report as the 'end of the party' for them personally and respond very aggressively indeed.

The surveys generally reflect honest opinion. Of course, you can get skewed results if people are very dissatisfied with one particular issue and generalise their discontent across all their answers on all the subjects in question. It's important to meet as many people as possible one to one prior to carrying out anonymous surveys so you can both shape the questions and set up validation for the overall survey. Most people in organisations in the right friendly environment will be reasonably honest with an independent, charming and approachable interviewer. Some people are guarded, but most folks are quite open.

Sometimes the surveys demonstrate that the organisation is open, honest and efficient. They paint the picture of happy, hard working, contented and enlightened people, who enjoy coming to work, enjoy their work, enjoy the opportunity to mix with like-minded, pleasant people. These organisations are definitely out there and we work with a number of them.

Then there's the rest. Some are tolerable, some not so bad, some very bad, and some have set up such amazing 'cycles of abuse' that it's a miracle they get away with it, ethically financially, morally and legally.

How do I define cycles of abuse? It is the accumulation of verbal behaviours over time, resulting in the inability of a subordinate to deal with the verbal behaviours from above him or her in the organisation. This frequently leads people into the trap of having to find an outlet for their frustration, passing the abuse either down the line or to people with no connection to the organisation at all, including their family members. At whatever level this happens in the organisation, there is a good chance it will be passed on down the line further.

The accumulation of these cycles creates a generally aversive culture inside the local environments within the organisation. This leads to havens of learned helplessness where people will exhibit cynicism regarding the company and its individuals.

Learned Helplessness

*A condition of a human in which it has learned to behave helplessly, even when the opportunity is restored for it to help itself by avoiding an **unpleasant** or harmful circumstance to which it has been subjected.*

Martin E. P. Seligman

These verbal behaviours are very easy to spot in meetings. It's also easy to spot if a siege mentality has built up in groups; sometimes in projects you get groups of people in a generally aversive company environment still delivering great work. I have experienced this many times. You feel as if you and your team are still going to deliver the project despite the patronising nonsense you get from above.

I encounter people who are clearly suffering from cycles of abuse. Their main problem is often that they don't have anything to say back when they receive abuse from others. I have discussed long lists of possible things they could say as a retort.

Sadly, the relationship in question is usually mature and has fully developed, making a reversal unlikely without putting the victim in a position of peril (real or perceived). Sometimes, people who have received abuse just welcome any opportunity to talk about it.

Of course, the easiest way to deal with this kind of stress is to recognise it early on and nip it in the bud. The best way to do that is to think about this week's planned encounters, consider if any of them are likely to be stressful and prepare some retorts. This kind of preparation is quite easy and you can be pretty assured that no-one else is preparing for the week's verbal behaviour encounters, so you will be ahead of the game. You do not have to be that far ahead of the protagonist to be able to outsmart him, you really don't.

If you think you are likely to be subjected to ribbing or even verbal abuse (passive aggressive or aggressive), here are some retorts you could consider, or use to produce your own spectrum of possibilities. Of course, I have no idea of your environment or wider organisational culture, but all of these statements need to be delivered in a calm and adult manner:-

1.   I am sorry, but I do not accept the premise of your statement.
2.   I am sorry, but I do not accept the premise of your question.
3.   I am sorry, but we do not appear to be talking about efficiently delivering the business here.
4.   I am sorry, but if this is supposed to be motivating me, it isn't.
5.   I am sorry, but my view is that all the team here are trying to deliver the project. I do not appreciate the insinuations that we are not.
6.   I am sorry, but this kind of macho stuff does nothing for me at all.
7.   I am sorry, but I do not accept that creating internal friction is good for the delivery of the business/project.

8. Excuse me, but when you say they will get a 'kicking', do you mean a physical kicking?
9. Excuse me, but this does not feel like a strategic conversation, it feels like we are rummaging in the detail here; surely we have other people to debate this content?
10. I am sorry, but looking around the room, this does not feel like a happy place.
11. This dialogue appears to be designed to punish the very people we are relying on to deliver the business. Why would we want to do that?
12. It's getting noisy in here.
13. How would you all feel if we recorded these meetings in future?
14. Would you mind if I recorded our one-to-ones?
15. We appear to have made 'doing the right things' punishing and 'doing the wrong things' reinforcing; how did that happen?
16. We appear to be programmed to take the wrong things seriously and the right things lightly; how did we do that?
17. What do you think this meeting would look like if it was great?
18. I think I need to tell you that when you talk to me like that, I find it quite depressing and confidence sapping.
19. We appear to have been bullied into saying we could complete something we couldn't, and now we are being bullied because we haven't completed it.
20. You appear to be sniping at us, has someone else been subjecting you to extinction?
21. I am sorry, I will have to go now, I am badly in need of some adult conversation.

It's people's courage that will determine whether some of these statements will be said in their own work setting. Ironically their reticence may well be the thing that got them here in the first place. I have observed many 'sunflowers' rise through the ranks in organisations only to fail at the level where they should have demonstrated courage to get to the next step. By this time, they have been shaped into submissiveness by the very leaders that should have ensured that they were courageous.

If you are successful at your job, most bosses (good and bad alike) will allow you an amazing number of mistakes and idiosyncrasies. Most egotistical leaders are not so stupid as to punish you if you are very obviously successful at your job. If you feel inspired and have the courage of your convictions and the data to back them up, then what are you waiting for?

14. I've just realised I am part of the problem, a big part

Each relationship you have comprises many encounters which, over time, produce a very predictable set of verbal behaviours back and forth. You are a major shareholder in these relationships; you need to take care with what you say and how you respond to things. If you heard some words in the past that you did not appreciate and ignored them, then you probably set yourself on the road to a dysfunctional relationship of some kind.

Here is a question I am frequently asked by clients: "What can I do if this daft stuff has been going on for many years and I haven't said anything? If I say something now, I am going to look really stupid." Well, you may feel stupid, and there's a good chance your guilt will be impacting other things in your life as well. The real question now is, bearing in mind this has been going on for years and you are now at step forty six: How do you get back to step minus ten?

For sure, past behaviour is a very good predictor of future behaviour. Someone's responses to a long-standing protagonist are likely to have been well conditioned over time. All is not lost. It is quite possible to produce a shaping plan that can take someone back to a place where they can deliver differing responses over time and receive different consequences in the future. The hard part in coaching this kind of circumstance is getting the client to focus on the goal. Usually, they are focused on the many injustices they feel have been meted out to them over the years. I will commonly say, "Could you just look on this as a stand-alone distinct project, with activities, reviews, adjustments and all the usual elements of a project? Yes, it seems 'over the top' for a fix on a dysfunctional relationship but tell me again how long has this been driving you crazy?"

In our personal lives we have the freedom to end relationships and remove ourselves from the same environment as people we don't like. There is a strong perception that there's just no escape from idiots at work and that's why so many people resort to learned helplessness.

I suspect that we pay much more attention to the little details in our personal relationships, at least in the early stages of a relationship. We are constantly watching for signs that will confirm (or not) how we think the relationship is going. We also have an emotional element to our personal lives that probably does not exist at work.

For example, you go out for a first date. You look for signs that you resonate with the other person and them with you. You get encouraging signs. You go on the second date, you test out the delivery and response of certain behaviours, you adjust, and you constantly look for signs. You keep the relationship going or dump him or her. It's all observation, founded on looking for signs of resonance and trust. We don't do any of this type of experimentation at work. In fact we shy away from it; "my dysfunctional boss keeps making irritating and patronising comments; I wish I could dump him, I certainly don't trust him."

At work, a hierarchical system encourages the high-ups to think they don't have to treat subordinates as they would treat valued customers. If you could wave a magic wand, perhaps this is the one thing you could reverse to ensure people take care of key relationships at work.

What could you do now, having read this message?

Look out for the potential to move your workplace relationships to a different footing. People around you are talking to you (behaviour), they are talking about you (behaviour), they are responding to your messages (behaviour). You are drowned in the potential to observe the behaviours of those around you. Pick one or two and have a think about what you could do and say differently. It has to be different in order to change your relationship with this person. It doesn't have to be a massive difference and it doesn't have to be emotional; just different.

There's a good chance you can't think of anything to say. Think about someone you know; not the worst person in your circle, someone who may be co-operative, someone you like. Wait for your opportunity to respond differently to that person. Most verbal behaviours are repeated again and again so you have lots of time to pick a good one. When you have decided on your 'different' response, deliver it. See what happens – that's it. Yes, this is not complex.

Be vigilant. If someone else is out to marginalise you, you need some responses in hand and the courage to deliver them when you get the opportunity.

15. Are we on the same page here?

I surprised myself this year; I was convinced that some leaders were not doing what they should be doing because they were having too much fun doing lots of the wrong stuff. It wasn't true. They weren't doing the right stuff because they didn't know what it was, or how to do it. I had been talking to them about poor results, other operational problems, low levels of good feedback and all kinds of other stuff. I came to understand that I had missed out a number of shaping steps in my coaching. The problem turned out to be that they didn't know what to say to people. We agreed some things they could say and everything started to change. It's a bit embarrassing for us all now, we had all thought the solutions were complex but no, we were just short of a few lines.

In the leadership arena nearly all the behaviours are verbal; it's the words, the actual words, in the right order, delivered with the right amount of consideration and sincerity that make the difference.

If we were making a sales pitch to a new potential client we would probably follow a process starting with a set of questions like this:-

1. In your view is your organisation running at 100% efficiency?
2. Are your people delivering 100% discretionary effort aligned to success?

3. Are you worried that people don't have enough time to complete the basics of their jobs?
4. Do you have many meetings?
5. Do people fail to deliver on time and to the right quality?
6. Do you think you are 'too busy' most of the time?
7. Do you get a lot of surprises?
8. Do you go 'off site' in order to ensure you have enough thinking time?

If the meeting is affable then I would expect most of the answers to these questions to be 'no'. On further questioning, I would then expect the client to talk about certain individuals who are not performing (they usually do). I have never encountered anyone who said, "It's all my fault, I am in charge of this ship and I have created a culture that has resulted in all my answers to the above to be in the negative, I'll get my coat, tell my wife I love her....."

You might ask – 'So the first time someone strategically considers where they are and where their business sits is when you turn up and ask a bunch of simple questions?' The answer is 'yes', but you can't be surprised; when was the last time you did it? You could write down all that is right and wrong with your career/life right now; stop reading and do it now. But we don't. We have set up a mesmerising mass of daily behaviours and we are diligently working our way through them, burning up precious time. Our life is made up of discreet periods of time all packaged together. You only get one life; how often do you stop and consider if this current course is acceptable to you?

People rarely stop for reflection. I have advised many people to go for a walk in the morning instead of zooming off to be in the office for 7am. A sensible breakfast followed by a nice walk, using the time for reflection, thinking about what's happening, how they could be approaching all the things that are imminent, what's the best strategy etc. Most people would rather steam through their calendar-created activities with little consideration about genuine business-led priorities or the effect they are having on others. I am recommending more thinking and less improvising on a theme. 'Less is more' for sure.

I have been coaching for many years and yes, almost all of the things I say to my clients are very obvious and there for anyone to see if they just look for them. So why do people make things so hard for themselves if it's all obvious? I really don't know, but they do. We all do, I do. We maybe want to protect our self image and reject anything we think is a threat. The relieving thing about using behavioural science is that we can focus on what people do and say, and not have to worry about their thoughts, agendas, fears, and all that other stuff in the deep recesses of their closet. It is also less threatening to us because we don't have to know the answer right away. We are expecting to be iterating for some time. It creates the environment where we are allowed to make mistakes and get better and better......and better.

16. Epilogue

The final chapter of this book is a set of related stories. The similarities lie in the typically flawed assumptions made by the corporate protagonists involved. If I could wave a magic wand, I would immediately create an understanding within all organisations of the value of:-

1. The need for repetition and practice in all training.
2. Engaging the workforce in setting business targets.
3. The true value to organisations of accurate and honest feedback.
4. The effect calm leaders can have in setting clear expectations.
5. The increase in useful information from frequent, simple opinion surveys.
6. The desperate need to reduce spookology in HR processes.
7. The importance of shaping and clear, deliverable goals.
8. The part behavioural science can play in avoiding overfacing everyone.

a. The answer lies in the repetition

A concert is the opportunity for you to see your favourite musicians and singers perform. You want them to sing your favourite songs, the ones you listen to again and again on your iPod. As James Taylor sang, "People pay money, to hear 'Fire and Rain', again and again and again."

Some people view a management conference as something different from a concert. A management conference is a set of speeches and presentations. I believe it's supposed to be interesting and entertaining; if it's inspiring then that's just fantastic. Some folks are insulted if they hear the same speech twice and so some great speeches and presentations suffer from the paradigm that they must be unique. This is odd. If the original was fantastic, then the revision could be even better. I've seen Billy Connolly a number of times and I am happy if he repeats something I have heard him do before. I must be happy; I'm laughing. In the same way, I have seen some speakers give the same speech many times, for many years. Some are great every time and some of them give speech-making a bad name.

The same paradigm applies to training courses that introduce people to a new skill. Training like this is designed to get people started on their learning journey, but sometimes it gets translated into a binary state where they are measured on whether they attended the training or not, rather than considering what was learned. I've attended behavioural science courses many times. I like them, I'm still learning, it's why I am doing the courses. I am not slow; well not any slower than anyone else.

Some repetition is accepted without question; for example, if you are learning how to play the guitar or how to swing a golf club. The need for repetition is not so readily accepted as essential when it comes to training courses. 'I attended, therefore I've learnt the course material' is a nonsensical position that doesn't stand up to much scrutiny.

If people are attending a course in order to learn some new skills, then how much they practise will be the dependent factor on their success with the course. Many repetitions are required if we want to learn a new skill to a level of competency. There is a world of difference between reading a book, attending a training course or conference and actually practising some new skills – it's the whole game, in fact it's the only game in town.

b. How to create mistrust with workers

Here is a sure-fire popular pastime that creates mistrust within
organisations. Firstly, the directors decide what targets they
actually want to achieve for the year. Then, they exaggerate these
targets to an improbable, much higher level in the belief that
people will fail and only achieve the level that they decided in
private. The directors will then hold road shows to roll out the
exaggerated targets for the year with flash and enthusiasm.
They'll set up new ways for people to report on progress. All very
optimistic in the early stages - lots of smiling and upbeat talk.

There is, of course, a reality. As the year slouches along,
directors get more and more irritated by their perceived non-
compliance within the organisation. Blame appears on the scene
just around the time it looks like the targets will not be
achieved. Anger appears when even their secret original targets
look unachievable. Why does this happen?

The people within the organisation whose task it is to deliver
results were never in on the decision to set the targets initially.
They probably looked on the exaggerated targets with disdain,
realising from the start that they were unachievable, and
instantly felt disengaged from the process. Ironically, then, the
very people employed to deliver the heart of the business never
knew what their true goals were. This is deceit on a massive
scale. It happens frequently and it's a very popular process.
Why do some organisations perform this pantomime year in
year out?

I have a piece of paper with three words on it which I use a
lot in workshops. The words are: Aspiration, Opinion and Data.
In conversation with people I frequently say, "Can I stop you
there? Was what you just said an aspiration, your opinion or do
you have some data to back that up?" More often than not the

response is, "Well, I suppose I haven't been counting, no." Let's just stop this film right now and pause for thought!

Consulting the performer and asking him or her, "What can be realistically achieved?" is the key to success and also a good motivator. The leader's job is to create conditions for success.

c. Better a comfortable delusion than a cruel truth.

I frequently speak to people that tell me they are robust and can take any kind of feedback. They tell me they want to learn more, improve their work performance, be a better parent, the whole nine yards. They laugh along when I give them examples of the antics ofsome clueless deluded managers, data on the numbers of engaged and disengaged people in organisations... oh how they laugh!

Most people are overly confident about their ability to receive tough feedback. Imagine someone gets drunk, bravado ensues, they claim they can hold their hand over a naked flame for 10 seconds; they put their hand close to the flame, scream out loud and look for some ice. Feedback is one of those things that attracts a good level of bravado. Most people think that they are robust. It turns out hardly anyone is in the slightest way robust. A better description would be 'really sensitive to anything that might go against their self image'. In fact, anything that even remotely looks like it's going against their self image.

The paradox, when it comes to feedback, is that perfectly honest and pleasant people will, from time to time, claim something about themselves which is clearly not true to most observers. Others in their vicinity cringe when they hear these outrageous aspirational statements but say nothing to correct it. There are many reasons why we will not contradict something we know to be untrue. Not speaking out, however, means that the untrue statements will keep occurring, even get worse. Here are some perfectly reasonable reasons and rationalisations for staying silent: "It's not worth the hassle," "I couldn't care less," "I've got a mortgage to pay, you know."

You may well hear aspirational statements made from time to time in organisations about how "honest and robust" we are, about "how great our company is," about how we are "simply the best." Common responses include inwardly looking to the sky and inwardly tutting. I believe people when they say, "I want to change for the better." This is from their current position of relative comfort. Coming to terms with just how hard it is to embark on a journey of genuine discovery is step one. Sadly, most people ignore the need for the steps before step one and bypass this crucial stage, coming a cropper when the whole thing becomes too overwhelming.

d. The conundrum of worker engagement

Here are some common concerns I have heard from leaders:-

"I work hard, I am in a position of responsibility, I am a good leader, I am not scary at all, I am calm, I say hello to everyone, I am respectful and polite. So how come I can't get people to do what I want them to do?"

"I take great pains to plan my work, I think about work all the time, driving in my car, doing the dishes, mowing the lawn, I have many ideas, I communicate with everyone regularly, I have good communication tools, email, blackberry, so why won't they do what I want? Why am I constantly let down by the perfectly able people that I like?"

"It can't be me that's at fault can it? Do you think I need to hire some better talent?"

I've already talked at length about the fact that the workplace environment drives behaviour, that you are perfectly designed to get what you currently get, that if you are the leader you get precisely what you deserve, that everything currently happening around you happens for a reason.

I am old, I have watched great leaders, I have seen them work magic. They set very clear expectations (not detailed - clear). They are calm, polite, they are available to speak to, they have tidy desks, they are scary and yet exciting to be around. They don't actually say that much. They keep things very simple, they listen, you can tell that they listen; they listen to you and then do things that impress you. You feel a respect and security that they listened to you. It feels good, you are confident; you start listening more to your people, more of the right things start to happen. You don't over-react anymore when something goes wrong.

Yes, you may have to say to someone, "Look I need you to come and see me in my office tomorrow. I'll tell you what it's about when you come." When they arrive in your office you may say something like, "Sorry, but this isn't going to be a conversation; I will speak and then I want you to leave and think about what I said. I specifically asked for you to deliver [something] by Wednesday. You said I'd get it and I didn't. I don't want this to happen again, please."

When it comes down to it, you have to do this kind of thing. Probably not often, but you must follow up if things don't get delivered. Once you let stuff go then no-one really knows what you want or by when. That's what keeping things simple means. Set clear expectations and provide appropriate consequences for people. Effective leadership is most definitely not complex.

e. Staff culture surveys

I once had a conversation with the CEO of a very big UK
company; it was centred on their annual staff culture survey. We
were reviewing their previous year's survey and he was concerned
that it didn't really tell him anything apart from the 600 or so
written statements each person had filled in on the free text box at
the end of the exhaustive and bemusing 150 tick-box questions.
I asked what it was he was looking for. He wanted to know what
the staff thought he should be doing to improve efficiency,
customer service and general staff satisfaction and happiness.

I suggested instead that they run a 10 question survey and spend
some time thinking what ten questions they would like answers
to. They could run this on a three-monthly basis and make a
statement following each one; mainly it would be an opportunity
to apologise for all the things people complained about and start
to fix some of the broken processes. The CEO would then have
an opportunity to create some trust, which would enable him to
find out the truth he was looking for. If they stuck to the same
survey they could show improvements over time. It would be
transparent, it would deliver what he wanted.

After a long debate round and round the objectives, potential
outputs and the simplicity of doing less, but more frequently, they
decided to continue doing exactly what they had done every other
year. The prospect of anyone finding dysfunction, dissatisfaction or
weaknesses in their processes was too threatening. Their sensitivity
to the City, their share price, the thought of what they might find
looking for the blunt truth were enough to get them to carry on with
the voluminous and complex externally bought-in online survey.

This kind of corporate cowardice is more common than you
would think. In this case, the CEO said at the end, "Do you
realise that there is no way we can have a satisfaction score

lower than the previous year? There are many things we cannot control when it comes to our share price and this isn't one of them. We have to lock this thing down and ensure we get another modest improvement across the whole business."

f. Stereotyping

I am often asked to comment on company development plans which are predicated on psychological tests. If I'm being kind, these are overly complex. If I'm feeling less generous, they are utterly bemusing.

I don't need a set of psychometrics to tell me my personality type and I certainly don't want to be shoe-horned into some psychologist's '16 stereotypes'. I am an individual; I have my own unique behavioural patterns which change depending on whether I am in my office on my own, in someone else's office with others, at a conference, on a train - you get my point.

My behaviour is contingent on whatever local environment I am part of; I operate on that particular environment. I have a personality, yes; we are pretty much stuck with that. I also have a life history of experiences. The cello section of the London Symphony Orchestra have different personalities but for sure they play beautiful music; that's what we pay for, that's what they're paid for.

I don't think we need to use a tool to predict what people might do at work. Most of our colleagues have been around for a while, behaving every day; we can already observe what they are actually doing and saying. Everyone I know at work already has a view on me and my behaviour. I am aware of some of their opinions about me and I am unaware of other aspects of it. I could sit down now and write a list of everyone I know. I could write some comments of what I think of them. Some they'll know already, some they won't. Why is that?

The use of the psychology tool box in business has led to some people actually using their test results to justify the idiosyncratic elements of their day to day behaviours. There were three instances of this recently: "If you knew my personality type then you would realise why I didn't ring you back." "You've already told me five things; the research says that's all we can remember." "You should be aware I am an ENTJ; we are natural leaders. I am sorry, but my aggression is typical ENTJ fallout." I am sorry, too: This stuff has been around for so long now that people have started to believe it to be right.

My colleague, Dr Nicole Gravina said:

I think a glaring problem with personality tests is that we take them for ourselves without the opinions of others. So, our answers are our idealized versions of ourselves. Therefore, when we take them we aren't learning about anything in our blind spot, we're only fanning our own egos. It would be much more interesting if people around us took a personality test about us.

I know a famous personality researcher. He told a story about how, many years ago, they wanted to come up with a better way to select students into the clinical psychology program. They thought they could use their personality to predict being a good clinician and they assumed that ENTJs were the best. So, they got a big grant and conducted a study comparing clinician (psychologist) performance to their personality and they couldn't find a link. They changed the way they measured performance three times and still couldn't find a link. It turns out that being a good clinician is based on what you do and say every day, not personality. I like this story because even a famous personality researcher had to admit that they couldn't find a link in the workplace most relevant to them.

Psychology says that behaviour is contingent on personality. Behavioural science says it's contingent on environment. The successful training and coaching of people is about having accurate, pinpointed data and delivering the resulting feedback so skilfully that you achieve an improvement in each performer. Everyone should receive skilfully-delivered, useful, simple feedback on their performance. If you use behavioural science, you really don't want to mix in psychology: it's counterproductive, it's mixing objective and subjective, it's never going to make any sense.

The workplace is in homeostasis: All the behaviours by all of the people are occurring in similar patterns every day. All these behaviours can be observed, and the effects of them can be observed and analysed. Using behavioural science to improve business works, it works very well. It's simple, but not easy. It will require a number of people to face up to their feedback. It will show that some people are causing all kinds of damage. It will show that a few people are driving the vast majority of wealth creation. It will demand that people are honest. It will argue that a number of corporate norms are counterproductive. It will deliver data that a number of cherished activities add no value. It will deliver data that some previously unrecognised people really do need a pat on the back.

Where do we start? Well empathy is the tool that creates engagement, even amongst groups of people hardened by years of failed initiatives. Run some surveys, ask the right questions, don't over-face, ask for written comments, publish the lot and apologise for what went before. This should give you the chance to create a new way forward, based on creating the right workplace environment where all personality types can thrive.

g. A Success Story

I recently met someone I had not seen since I delivered a course to his management team some two years ago. His graduation improvement plan had been to increase the percentage of planned maintenance for his numerous industrial plants. His company had a global target of 80% 'planned' to 20% 'reactive' maintenance ratio. The first thing he did was find out what the actual 'planned' rate was (warts and all) and it came in at a disappointing 33%. He also calculated that the cost of maintaining plants in a reactive way, including the disruption of breakdowns etc was four times the cost of a 'planned' regime. He asked that the global 80% target be dropped closer to the actual rate so the 'greyhound could see the hare he was supposed to be chasing' and received a terse 'no' from his corporate masters.

Unabashed, he set out to improve the 'planned' rate. He did this by visiting plants and suggesting to his plant managers that they get together with their teams and simply ask them, "How could we increase the planned maintenance rate?" then sit back and listen to their ideas. He asked them to take notes, especially the 'reasons why we can't.........' He met the plant managers again a month later and they went through the lists of ideas and apparent blocks to progress. They removed a number of blocks, changed a few standing orders, amended some processes and went forward with a new vigour to get the planned maintenance rate up. This was a brilliant example of setting some new simple expectations and shaping to an ambitious goal one step at a time. They agreed an 'unofficial' goal of 36% planned for the first month and exceeded it by two percentage points.

Two years on, the planned rate is now 78%, still 2% short of the corporate target. He has still not received any bonus for planned maintenance despite this massive improvement. Nevertheless, he is very happy; he has applied the pinpointing and shaping principles from his BMT course and improved his business. He is applying the same simple principles to a number of other aspects of his business now and others in the organisation have noticed something is going on.

Over a two year period, he has impacted on the workplace environment dramatically. Many people now have an improved daily work experience. He has removed the uncertainty of being massively adrift from the company KPI's, he has introduced a much more 'bottom up' approach to problem-solving. It's not magic, it's science; it's a simple set of logical steps leading gradually toward an achievable goal.

Ironically, even though the company clearly is benefitting from his ingenuity, they still try to manage him through 'top down' edicts. He has created an umbrella where, above him, the old ways still exist. Below him in the organisation however, things are very different. The real shame is that the leaders are unaware of what he's done. Even after he has explained it, they will not credit him. They will more probably take the credit for it and base the success on their dubious corporate processes; any port in a storm. That, my friend, is what you should expect business to be like without proper leadership. These leaders are not stupid; they are distracted - which makes them look stupid.

h. The irresistible temptation to use multiple antecedents

Businesses overuse antecedents. An antecedent is an attempt to stimulate a behaviour. It's crucial that one exists, or people may not know what to do, but antecedents are poor at driving the desired behaviour unless attendant consequences are applied. The world is full of antecedents; most of them don't work very well.

Consequences drive behaviour. Machines do most of what they're supposed to do, most of the time – machines don't need consequences to work; humans do. Expecting humans to act like machines is unwise.

It's very difficult to get folks to stop just writing down a process and making the fatal mistake of thinking that humans will follow the process. It's only ever going to be true if the consequences for the behaviour are aligned for the performer to carry out that behaviour. You could test any process to see how often it is being carried out. I have said many times that 'processes' are the hard components and 'behaviours' are the soft skills. It is very easy to write rules, procedures, laws etc. It is very difficult to create the conditions where people will adhere to them. Some basic rules here:-

1. People prefer to decide the 'how it will be done' themselves.
2. Not many people like being 'supervised', especially if the supervisor is a prat.
3. People like to be trusted to get on with their job.
4. People need to feel that the responsibility of doing their job is on their shoulders.
5. Leaders can design work teams that will deliver business/projects.
6. People in teams can also design successful teams.
7. Organisation charts can restrict good sense in business.
8. Company rules can stifle creativity; adapt them accordingly.
9. Try to avoid creating an organisation where doing the right thing is impossible.
10. If you make suggestions to fix procedures, one a week per person would change an organisation in a year.
11. Regular honest feedback gives you the full field of current activity – your decisions will be based on fact.
12. Create opportunity for frequent honest feedback; don't worry about it having to be anonymous.

17. And finally...

A comprehensive understanding of the effect of consequences can change your life, dramatically. This final step in the book was written by my good friend Nicole Gravina. She wrote the excellent foreword to the book and has given me permission to place this piece of wisdom here at the end of the book. The reason I would like you to read this is that it demonstrates beautifully just how powerful an understanding of the science of behaviour can be. Nicole also demonstrates that behavioural terminology does not have to be mystical and it can be used to explain simple day to day situations.

The Biology of Reinforcement and Punishment

You may have heard of the 4:1 rule; we should deliver four positive pieces of feedback for every constructive one. This recommendation is based in scientific research. Effective teachers follow this rule. So do high performing teams. Even happy marriages seem to follow this pattern. In fact, in some cases, the suggested ratio is even higher. In courses, I ask the class what they think the ratio is for marriages that end in divorce and they tend to guess 1:4 but research says that a 1:1 ratio is enough to steer people toward the divorce court.

Why do we need so much more positive reinforcement? The answer is probably in our DNA.

Reinforcement

Back in our caveman days, we benefited from short acting effects of reinforcement. When we found a piece of fruit that was delicious and nutritious, our behaviour of going to that spot to find food was reinforced. But if that reinforcement sustained for too long and we didn't find food there again for a while but continued to look, we might have ended up starving. We needed reinforcement to be short-lived so we would try something new if the previous behaviour wasn't working. It turns out that short-lived reinforcement makes our behaviour more agile, we adjust based on where we are getting reinforcement.

Sometimes it can be frustrating to have to deliver so much reinforcement to shape behaviour and keep it going, but the upside is that it means we can change behaviour fast.

Punishment

In contrast, cavemen and cavewomen benefitted from punishment having a long lasting effect. If they ate something that made them sick, it was good for them to have an aversion to it for a long time, it helped them stay healthy. If the impact of punishment was fleeting and they needed to keep testing to learn that something was bad for them, they probably weren't going to live for very long.

The short duration of reinforcement effects and the long duration of punishment effects was very functional for us back in our hunter gatherer days, but it is probably less functional for us today. Yet, this tendency still impacts us now. If most of our interactions with our boss are positive and just a few are negative, those few negative ones hold a lot of weight, maybe more than what seems logically fair from the boss's perspective.

In addition, if our spouse screws up, we might be more likely to rehash the event a few years later than we would be to remember the nice thing they did for us the day before. This means we have to be really careful about how much punishment we deliver to others. The long lasting effects of punishment can *sometimes result in substantial damage to a relationship that takes an enormous effort to repair. Of course, acknowledging the misstep and apologizing can make that process move much more quickly.*

Sometimes it can be frustrating to have to deliver so much reinforcement to shape behaviour and keep it going, but the advantage is that we can change behaviour fast. This agility has allowed us to progress and advance over time. It's why we learn new things and take on new challenges. Understanding that we all have the power to change our own and others' behaviour, for better or worse, is the very first step before step one.

Dr Nicole Gravina

Appendix A

Behavioural science terms used in this booklet

Behavioural science is the science of human behaviour; it is founded on using data and analysis to come to conclusions about what is happening in the interactions of people. Objectivity is at the core of behavioural science. Behavioural Management Techniques (BMT), is a blend of behavioural science tools and project management skills.

I have written a booklet called 'Notes on Behavioural Management Techniques' which discusses behavioural terms and offers more explanation than is covered here. This chapter should be enough to help you with the terms I mention in this booklet.

Psychology seeks to understand what is going on inside the mind, to modify these internal phenomena and in doing so achieve behaviour change. Behavioural science observes the behaviour, seeks to modify the external environment, which is the only thing we really have influence over anyway, and in doing so achieve behaviour change. Behavioural science sees each person as an individual who desires a totally unique set of reinforcers from their environment (their world).

Both mainstream psychology and behavioural science are used in seeking to change behaviour. Critically, behavioural science has a greater verifiable record of achieving this and is also far easier for people to learn and apply.

A number of scientific terms are used in this booklet. These are simply described here: -

Antecedents

An antecedent is a request or prompt, something which is attempting to drive a particular behaviour. A sign that says 'don't smoke', a speed sign, and a plan detailing how you will deliver a project are all antecedents. Antecedents are quite poor at driving behaviour if they are not paired with consequences. We are all regularly bombarded with antecedents.

Some antecedents are very good at delivering what's intended. I care about the weather forecast the day before I'm going on a long walk. I care about the flight information board when I'm flying somewhere. I check what day I have to put the bins out. I look at the fuel gauge in my car when driving. Unfortunately, many work-based antecedents do not have the desired effect. Procedures, safety rules, notice boards, minutes of meetings and requests by email will all work in part, but will only work well if paired with consequences.

Consequences

The impact of consequences is the primary effect on our behaviour. What happens to us following our behaviour will affect the likelihood of us performing the same behaviour again under similar circumstances.

Behavioural science states that there are two main consequence types that result in a behaviour occurring/recurring or stopping. They are defined as Reinforcement and Punishment. These fundamental principles are as follows:-

• If behaviour is maintained or increases it has been subject to reinforcement.
• If behaviour reduces or stops it has been subjected to punishment.
• The consequence in each individual case is defined by its impact on behaviour.

Extinction

Extinction is the process of being ignored and can be very painful if you are the recipient of it. It is also a useful tool to use if you wish someone's irritating behaviour to go away. A subset of extinction is the extinction burst, an emotional outburst of some kind (usually verbal). This usually occurs when the behaviour is receding and is a good indicator that it is.

Environment

The environment is the immediate location of a person, be it in their office, living room, their car; wherever the behaviour is occurring. A person's behaviour is mostly driven by the consequences that follow the behaviour. The environment will dictate the consequences you experience and this includes the other people in the room, office etc. Small changes in environment can result in significant changes in the behaviour of an individual. The environment affects us and we affect the environment.

For example, imagine an office full of people. Take one person out of the office and replace them with a different person and the environment has changed. The change could be very significant depending on who left and who came in.

Pinpointing

Pinpointing is the process used to make sure that a behaviour is described accurately. Something is pinpointed when it complies with the following rules:-

1. It can be seen or heard.
2. It can be measured, counted etc.
3. Two people would always agree that the behaviour occurred or not.
4. It is active (something is occurring).

People who learn pinpointing can quickly develop skills which reduce the amount of assumption in their environment. This reduction of (sometimes destructive) assumptions increases the amount of informed comment, decision and discussion.

It is advisable to gather data on situations via observations and keep notes of who actually said/did what. This significantly reduces the chance of unnecessary conflict created by assumption.

Pinpointing is a very useful skill for business. Next time someone relates something to you, if you are unsure of the message you can say, "Can you pinpoint that for me please?"

Shaping

Shaping is a simple concept which is very difficult to master. It recognises that you can't get from step one to step ten in one vertical stride. You sometimes have to first write out steps 2 through 9 and then carry them all out, one step at a time.

People sometimes tell me, "I want to say this to my boss." Before you say anything you need to predict the chances of it being received the right way by your boss. "Not very good," will often be the reply. Unfortunately, you have to shape to the goal you want to achieve, and this usually means a time-consuming set of steps which will shape the environment so that you can actually say what you want to say and it will have the desired effect.

Shaping is not for the impatient, and a realisation that patience is the key can take some people some time. Sometimes, there is no other choice. You can't force the situation to move any faster so your options are slow shaping or nothing. Many very reinforcing tools we use these days do not help us forge a patient approach, e.g. email and voicemail. It is reinforcing

working through a list of tasks, ticking actions off as you go.
It is not naturally reinforcing taking the extra time to consider,
"Is this the right thing to say? Does something else have to be
achieved before I can say this and get what I want?"

Shaping is inherent in everything we learn. If you want to play
an instrument, you repeat and repeat until you can play the tune.
Anything that requires mastery requires repetition. Putting a
group of employees to work effectively and safely requires a
leader to choose carefully who will work with whom. It requires
trial and error to find the best combinations. Iteration is trying
things out and seeing what the result is, adjusting and trying
again – this is shaping, it works, it's the only thing that does
work when building a team. This is how you succeed at getting
all the right people on the bus, sat in the right seats.

Appendix B
Hollin Consulting Ltd

Hollin Consulting are a mature consulting organisation that deliver behavioural management techniques (BMT) training and coaching. BMT is a blend of applied behavioural science tools and project management skills and is used to improve business and safety performance.

Our training ethos is to teach the customer how to identify their problems and then help fix them using BMT. Our involvement is designed to fade over time as the client organisation learns these techniques through our 'train the trainer' programme.

Hollin Consulting have been assisting their clients in delivering spectacular results since 2004 and we deliver training which quickly produces efficiency savings to the customer. Individual improvement plans deliver the efficiencies and cash savings to the business. Once customers accept the premise that there are inefficiencies within their organisation, it is easy to accept the concept of investing in BMT in order to achieve better results.

Our courses are suitable for all hierarchical levels in organisations. They are individually shaped to suit each particular set of course attendees. BMT courses become more bespoke as each module is completed; as the trainers receive feedback from the course attendees, the course is adapted accordingly to maximise results.

More information regarding Hollin Consulting can be found at www.hollinconsulting.co.uk
Our partners in the USA are Reaching Results
www.reachingresults.com

BMT Federation

We set up the BMT Federation in 2004 and so far this disparate group of enthusiasts has done much to get behaviour to the world. We have a pretty impressive community where ideas and feedback are fired around the group on a daily basis. We share everything; our course slides, notes, questions to students, case studies, ideas, wisdom, experience and bitter regrets for the occasional dumb stuff we get caught up in. It's worked really well over the last 10 years; I hope it continues to do so as it expands. The balance of backgrounds of the members is diverse and the links into academia connect us to the very latest and best research.

The Federation mission is to get behaviour to the world. The purpose of the Federation is to allow current BMT practitioners access to a wider population of like-minded people who are engaged in applying BMT to improve their business and safety performance.

BMT conferences

For the last eight years the Federation has organised a major BMT conference in the UK, normally held in the spring, and for the last six years a Behavioural Safety conference has been held in the autumn. For the last two years we have also held conferences in the USA. The conferences provide an opportunity for speakers to present papers on their successes with BMT and safety.

There is usually a mix of keynote speeches from guest speakers, our clients and from the Federation members. There is always opportunity for discussion on a wide range of related BMT and safety topics.

**For more information, log on to www.hollinconsulting.co.uk/conferences
Follow us on LinkedIn by joining the Behavioral Management Techniques for Leaders (BMT) group.**

Appendix C
Other Hollin books

THE TOO BUSY TRAP
By Howard Lees
ISBN number 978-0-9563114-7-4
£6.50

HOW TO EMPTY THE TOO HARD BOX, 2nd Edition
By Howard Lees
ISBN number 978-0-9563114-4-3
£6.50

HOW TO ESCAPE FROM CLOUD CUCKOO LAND, 2nd EDITION
By Howard Lees
ISBN number 978-0-9563114-8-1
£6.50

NOTES ON BEHAVIOURAL MANAGEMENT TECHNIQUES, 3rd EDITION
By Howard Lees
ISBN number 978-0-9563114-1-2
£6.50

IDEAS FOR WIMPS
By Howard Lees
ISBN number 978-0-9563114-6-7
£12.00

BEHAVIOURAL COACHING, 2ND EDITION
By Howard Lees
ISBN number 978-0-9563114-2-9
£6.50

BEHAVIOURAL SAFETY FOR LEADERS
By Howard Lees and Bob Cummins
ISBN number 978-0-9563114-5-0
£6.50

www.hollinconsulting.co.uk

notes: